W9-AOP-266

The Secret Lives of

Tigers

by Julia Barnes

GARETH**STEVENS**

GS

PUBLISHING
A Member of the WRC Media Family of Companies

Please visit our web site at: www.garethstevens.com
For a free color catalog describing Gareth Stevens Publishing's list of high-quality books
and multimedia programs, call 1-800-542-2595 (USA) or 1-800-387-3178 (Canada).
Gareth Stevens Publishing's fax: (414) 332-3567.

Library of Congress Cataloging-in-Publication Data

Barnes, Julia, 1955-
    The secret lives of tigers / Julia Barnes.
       p. cm. — (The secret lives of animals)
    Includes bibliographical references and index.
    ISBN–13: 978-0-8368-7659-8 (lib. bdg.)
    1. Tigers—Juvenile literature.   I. Title.
   QL737.C23B264   2007
   599.756—dc22   2006035329

This North American edition first published in 2007 by
Gareth Stevens Publishing
A Member of the WRC Media Family of Companies
330 West Olive Street, Suite 100
Milwaukee, WI 53212 USA

Gareth Stevens editor: Gini Holland
Gareth Stevens designer: Kami M. Strunsee
Gareth Stevens art direction: Tammy West
Gareth Stevens production: Jessica Yanke and Robert Kraus

Photo credits: copyright © istockphoto.com: Nicolas Delafraye, front cover,
p. 23; Joe Stone p. 9; Steffen Foerster p. 12; eROMAZe p. 13; Charlie Wright p. 17;
Glenn Mason p. 18; Michael Lynch p. 19; kevdog818 p. 20; Stephanie Kuwasaki p. 22;
MiStock pp. 24, 25; Demonoid p. 26; Mark Schroy p. 27. All other images copyright
© Westline Publishing Limited.

Printed in the United States of America

1 2 3 4 5 6 7 8 9 10 10 09 08 07 06

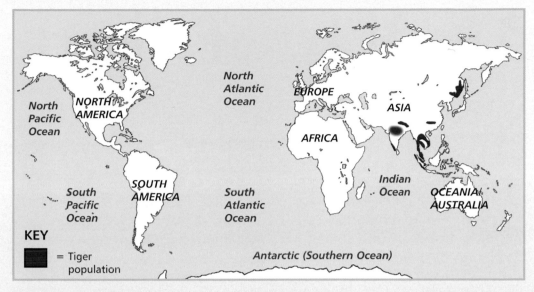

The worldwide population of tigers is confined to the continent of Asia, where tigers live in a variety of habitats.

of northwest India, and in the tall jungle grass at the foot of the Himalayas.

Why is the tiger such a great survivor?

- The tiger is a **solitary** animal and does not have to compete with other tigers for food.
- The tiger is the most skilled hunter on land, combining speed, power, and surprise.
- The tiger is equipped to be the most effective killer, armed with huge teeth and razor-sharp claws.
- The tiger has no natural enemies in the wild.

WHERE DO TIGERS LIVE?

The tiger has found a home in India, China, Russia, and countries in Southeast Asia. A number of different types of tigers have **evolved**. They are named according to where they come from. Some kinds of tigers are now **extinct**. The six kinds of tigers that still live in the wild are:

- The Indian or Bengal tiger.
- The Indo-Chinese tiger.
- The South China tiger.
- The Amur or Siberian tiger.
- The Sumatran tiger.
- The Malayan tiger.

The Ways of Tigers

The tiger is such a big, powerful, and skilled hunter that it does not need help from other tigers. All tigers, however, need some key things to survive in the wild.

FINDING A HOME
A tiger can be successful only if it has its own territory and does not have to compete with other tigers for food. A young tiger must find its own territory, and this may mean driving out an older, weaker tiger. Once it has its own territory, a tiger must defend the area from other tigers trying to find their own living spaces.

The size of the territory depends on how much **prey** there is to eat. In some parts of India, where

If there is good cover, a tiger can creep up on its prey without being seen.

Tigers need water to drink, but they also enjoy taking a dip or just splashing around.

plenty of prey live, a tiger may need only 60 square miles (155 square kilometers). In Siberia, where prey is scarce, a tiger's territory may be as large as 400 square miles (1,035 sq km).

The territory must have plenty of thick **cover** in the form of trees, bushes, or long grass. A tiger needs to **stalk** its prey, hiding in the undergrowth so it can launch a surprise attack.

FOOD AND WATER

The tiger hunts cattle, deer, and pigs. The Bengal tiger also tackles buffalo and antelope. Tigers prefer big game, but if big animals are scarce, tigers eat whatever game they can find, including snakes, monkeys, birds, and even fish when they can catch them.

As well as having enough to eat, a tiger needs watering holes within its territory. Watering holes are particularly important for tigers that live in hot climates. A tiger will take a dip in the heat of the day just to cool off.

A BREEDING PARTNER

All wild animals have a strong urge to find a partner and produce offspring, because this is the only way that its **species** will survive for future generations. Because the tiger lives alone, finding a mate is not always easy. A successful male will own a territory that has a number of smaller territories within it that belong to females. He will patrol his territory to keep **rival males** away from his breeding partners.

The Tiger's Perfect Body

The magnificent tiger has a body that is perfectly suited to its life as a meat-eating predator that relies on speed, power, and secrecy.

SIZE AND SHAPE

A tiger is a mighty animal, measuring about 6.5 feet (2 meters) long, and weighing about 507 pounds (230 kilograms).

The largest type of tiger, the Amur, or Siberian, tiger, can often weigh as much as 660 pounds (300 kg). The tiger's size and weight means that it can tackle large animals, which will provide the biggest feast from a single kill.

The tiger has the body of a super-fit, well-muscled athlete. To hunt, it runs at great speed over a short distance and then leaps onto the back of its prey, sinking in its razor-sharp teeth.

The tiger is also incredibly strong. After a kill, a tiger will often drag

Over a short distance, a tiger can reach speeds of 35 miles (56 km) per hour.

the **carcass** to a safe place before starting to eat.

COAT

A striped coat provides the perfect **camouflage** for a tiger that is creeping up on its prey. The tiger could be hunting in woodland, in the dappled sunlight in the jungle, or among the long jungle grasses in the foothills of the Himalayan Mountains. In these cases, the tiger's stripes blend in with grasses and low branches. The Amur tiger spends many months of the year in snow and is paler in color than the tigers of India and Malaysia, which live in the thick cover of the jungle. The pale color of the Amur tiger helps it blend into the snow as it stalks its prey.

TAIL

A tiger's tail is very long, measuring 3 to 4 feet (90 to 120 centimeters) in length, which is about half the length of the tiger's body. The tail is used for balance, especially when making tight turns at a high speed.

The tiger's canine teeth measure 3 inches (7.5 cm), which is the size of a person's middle finger!

CLAWS

The claws are 5 inches (12 cm) in length and are as sharp as knives. They are hooked, which allows the tiger to grasp a prey animal and stop it from escaping. The tiger can pull in its claws when they are not being used, which helps keep them sharp.

TEETH

The tiger kills its prey with a single bite of its huge **canine teeth**. The **incisor teeth** cut through the tough hide of a carcass and tear meat from the bones. The **molars** and **premolars** are used for slicing meat and for chewing.

How a Tiger Sees the World

Imagine yourself inside the body of a tiger. You walk on all four paws, have long, sharp claws and teeth, and a long tail. How does the world appear if you are the best meat-eating hunter on land?

EYESIGHT

A tiger has good vision both during the day and at night. During the day, a tiger can see as well as humans, but at night the tiger can see six times better than humans.

This tiger is on the alert, using its acute sense of hearing to pick up the slightest sound.

The spectacular whiskers are very sensitive, helping a tiger touch and investigate objects.

This better vision is because the tiger's eyes each have a special reflecting layer, which allows it to see in poor light. Tigers are also very skilled at judging distances, so a tiger can stalk an animal and then leap into action at exactly the right moment to catch and kill it.

HEARING

When a tiger is hunting, it relies far more on its hearing than on its eyesight or sense of smell. A tiger can tell the difference between the faintest rustle of leaves in the breeze and an animal brushing through the undergrowth. To a tiger, the snap of a twig is as loud as a rifle shot. Tigers can also detect high-pitched sounds that humans cannot hear.

SMELL

The tiger's sense of smell is not as well developed as that of a dog, but smell still has an important part to play in the tiger's world. The tiger will use its nose to track prey, but the main function of a tiger's nose is to read scent messages left by other tigers.

TOUCH

The tiger has long whiskers on its cheeks, above its eyes, and on its muzzle. These whiskers grow to about 6 inches (15 cm) in length, and they are used like our fingertips, so the tiger can feel for objects. A tiger's whiskers are especially important in helping the tiger sense how narrow an opening is on either side of it as it passes between rocks and trees.

11

Discovering Special skills

The tiger has the perfect body for a hunter, but it must also have the skills to find, follow, and attack its prey. It must make many decisions about how to move and when to strike. The tiger is a master of surprises, and its success as a hunter comes from its amazing ability know how to silently stalk its prey and then **ambush** it with a mighty leap and a killer bite.

STALKING

The tiger does not chase fast-moving animals, such as deer, for long distances,because running fast would use up too much energy and the tiger would be out-paced. A head-to-head fight with another animal would also be a bad plan, because the tiger might get injured. Instead, a tiger usually plays to its strengths. The tiger plans a hunt,

The tiger stalks its prey, moving silently step by step.

sometimes spending hours in preparation for a kill that will last seconds. When a tiger spots a likely **victim**, it will crouch down low and approach the animal step by step. If the prey animal hears, sees, or smells the tiger, it will take off in panic. The tiger moves, scarcely making a sound, always keeping downwind so its scent cannot be detected. If the prey animal looks up, the tiger will freeze and will become almost invisible, because its striped coat acts as the perfect camouflage.

The tiger is one of the most patient of hunters when stalking prey. A tiger may take 15 minutes to cover just 49 yards (45 m).

The tiger leaps into action, launching a surprise attack on its prey.

THE KILL

The tiger must get very close to its prey before attacking. It takes skill and experience for the tiger to figure out exactly the right moment to spring into action. If the tiger gets its timing wrong, the prey will run away and the hunt will end in failure. The tiger uses an explosive burst of speed to bound toward the prey animal and leap onto its back. In a split second, the tiger sinks its teeth into the animal's neck, killing it with a single bite.

SUCCESS AND FAILURE

Even though the tiger is a superb hunter, only one in twenty hunts that it attempts will be successful. For this reason, a tiger will feast on a kill, eating up to 77 pounds of meat (35 kg) in one sitting. It may have to go for several days before it can kill and eat again. In between successful hunts, it will be using a lot of energy searching for, and then stalking, its next meal.

13

What Does a Tiger Do All Day?

The tiger is a secretive animal and keeps itself well hidden. Scientists have had to go into the wild and spend long periods tracking and studying them to find out how tigers spend their time.

ON PATROL

A tiger will spend most of the day in the center of its territory, only leaving the area to patrol or to hunt. When a tiger goes on a patrol, it may have to walk long distances to reach the **boundaries** of its territory. The tiger will mark the boundaries with urine and droppings to warn off other tigers. It will also sniff round the boundaries to find out whether any tigers have come visiting.

WASHING

Tigers are very clean animals and will devote long periods each day to keeping their coats in good order. Like a pet cat, the tiger uses its tongue for grooming, licking its paws and wiping them over its face, ears, and forehead. An injured tiger will keep licking

A tiger patrols its territory, sometimes crossing wide stretches of water.

The tiger's day is divided between intense periods of activity and long periods of rest.

its wounds. This action keeps the cuts clean and also coats them with **antiseptic** saliva from the tiger's tongue.

KEEPING COOL

Tigers need fresh drinking water, so they need to visit a watering hole every day. In hot climates, the tiger will also use the water to cool off. A tiger may lie in a pool of water for an hour at a time. Tigers are also great swimmers. A tiger can swim across a river that is 4 miles (6.5 km) wide if it needs to reach another part of its own territory. Some tigers stalk their prey in water. The tiger will creep up on an animal, such as the water-loving sambar deer from India, and then attack it with a mighty splash.

SLEEPING

Tigers need a huge amount of energy for hunting, so they spend large periods of the day resting and sleeping. Scientists estimate that tigers sleep for sixteen to twenty hours each day.

HUNTING

The best time for hunting is just before the Sun has fully risen, and in the early evening as the light is fading. The tiger has excellent night vision and it can hunt in the late evening when it is almost dark. If its hunt is successful, the tiger will drag the carcass to a safe place and feast on it for hours.

How Do Tigers Communicate?

Tigers live alone, but they are in touch with other tigers on a regular basis, even though they rarely meet. Tigers have their own system of leaving secret signs, or messages, that other tigers can "read."

SECRET SIGNS
For tigers, scent is the best way of communicating with each other. A tiger that owns a territory must declare that the area has "no vacancies" to stop other tigers from trying to move in. Both male and female tigers need to do this, and they use the same method of making their mark along the boundaries of their territories.

• As a tiger patrols its territory, it sprays the bushes and trees along its path with a mixture of urine and liquid from a scent

This tiger scratches a tree, leaving behind a personal scent message.

16

gland at the base of the tail. This is a tiger's personal identification, and it shows that the tiger owns the territory.

- To make the message crystal clear, a tiger deposits droppings where they can be easily spotted.
- A tiger also has scent glands on its head and chin, and between its toes. Every time a tiger rubs or scratches against a tree or a branch, it leaves a personal scent message behind.

READING MESSAGES

A tiger must also "read" the messages that have been left by other tigers, as they contain vital information. When a tiger has found a scent, it tests it by using the **flehmen response**, which is sometimes known as the "stinking face." The tiger lifts its head, wrinkles its nose, and curls up its lips to open up the **Jacobson's organ**. This organ is a scent center in the roof of the tiger's mouth that is specially designed to test scents traveling through the air. By testing a scent a tiger can tell:

- If a tiger has come visiting.
- Whether the tiger has come this way before or is a stranger.
- The age of the visiting tiger.
- If the tiger is male or female.
- Whether a **tigress** in the area is ready for mating.

A TIGER'S VOICE

Tigers use their voices to communicate with each other, and this may be over long distances. At other times,

The stinking face: A tigress tests a scent using the flehmen response.

17

when tigers meet by chance, it is important that they make their feelings understood or the encounter could end in a fight. A mother tigress also needs to communicate with her cubs, and she has special sounds to communicate with them.

ROARING

Only big cats — the tiger, the lion, the jaguar, and the leopard — can roar. Tigers rarely roar. A roar is used when tigers communicate over long distances. A tiger may roar to warn other tigers to keep away, or, in the breeding season, a male may roar to attract females to his territory. A tiger's roar can be heard more than 1.8 miles (3 km) away. When roaring, a tiger will flatten its ears, wrinkle its nose, and narrow its eyes. Sometimes, a tiger will roar after a successful kill, but the attack itself is always carried out in silence.

GROWLS

A tiger growls deep in the back of its throat. This sound is a sign of aggression that says "I am about to attack."

SNARLS

The snarl sounds like a growl, but it often ends in hissing or spitting, which is very similar to the sound produced by people's pet cats. The tiger is saying: "Keep away!"

A tiger's mighty roar carries over long distances and warns other tigers to keep out of its territory.

A tiger flattens its ears and curls back its lips to give a menacing growl.

CHUFFING

This is a friendly sound, produced when a tiger closes its mouth and snorts through its nostrils. It is also known as "prusten," which, in German, means to sneeze or snort, or to burst out laughing. When two tigers meet on **neutral territory**, they will chuff to show that they do not regard each other as a threat.

POOK SOUNDS

The pook sound is very similar to the sound made by a sambar deer, which is a favorite prey animal of the tiger. Some experts think the tiger makes this sound so that the sambar will answer, revealing its whereabouts so the tiger can hunt it.

MOANS

Before a roar, a tiger may make a long, low, moaning noise. A mother and cubs will often "talk" to each other in soft moans.

GRUNTS

A mother tigress uses a special grunt that tells her cubs to follow her.

Times of Trouble

One secret of survival is to keep clear of trouble. People think of tigers as the most ferocious of animals, but they like to avoid fights if they can. A fight could result in injury, and this can spell disaster. If a tiger is injured and cannot hunt, it will starve to death. If it is able to hunt while its injuries heal, it still may die from infection.

FIGHTING TIGERS

Fights between tigers are rare, but they can be bloody contests. Tigers fight over territory, and two males may fight over a female in the breeding season.

When rival tigers meet, they snarl to show off their huge teeth, and they make themselves look as fierce as possible. An angry tiger holds its head low and twitches its tail.

If a tiger is old and weak, it may not want to risk fighting. In this case, the tiger needs to signal that it is giving in. A tiger does this by twisting its head and then rolling onto its back. In tiger

When two male tigers fight over a female, it may result in the death of one of the animals.

An old tiger that
is losing its powers
has a hard time
surviving in the wild.

language, this means: "I surrender." The winning tiger will take over the territory without having to fight.

If two tigers are evenly matched, they will fight, using their teeth and their claws as deadly weapons. A tiger may be badly wounded or even killed.

For a tiger living in the wild, an injury often leads to death, as the animal may no longer be able to hunt. So, even if a tiger kills a rival and wins the territory, it can die from wounds received in the fight.

OLD AGE
Life in the wild for an old tiger is very tough. In most cases, tigers live for ten to fifteen years. They survive much longer in zoos, often reaching twenty years of age, because they do not have to hunt for their food or defend a territory.

As a tiger becomes older, it loses its strength and speed. At this point, the tiger will have fewer successful hunts and the tiger will become weaker for two main reasons. First, it will have less food. Second, it will have to work harder to hunt for the prey it is able to kill. This is the ideal moment for a young, fit tiger to challenge the older tiger for its territory. A tiger that loses its territory cannot survive for long in the wild.

When Tigers Are Ready to Breed

We know that having a breeding partner is a top priority for tigers. So how do solitary animals manage to find each other?

GIVING SIGNALS

A tigress is ready to breed from about three to five years of age. A male is able to breed at the same age, but it may take him some time to establish a territory. Most tigers can breed at any time during the year, except Amur tigers, which mate over two months, between December and January.

A female advertises that she is ready for breeding by marking the boundaries of her territory. She also roars to alert male tigers in the area. A male tiger knows where females have their territories. If he picks up a scent message telling him that a female is ready for breeding, he quickly makes his way to her territory.

TIME TOGETHER

When a male and a female meet, they must first make it clear that their intentions are friendly. The tigers "talk" to each other using

In the breeding season, a solitary tiger will go in search of a partner.

the chuffing sound, and they will rub up against each other's bodies. The two tigers stay together for no more than a couple of days before the male returns to his territory.

The female tiger is **pregnant** for only fifteen to sixteen weeks. This period is a very short time compared with the amount of time that most large **mammals** are pregnant, but tigers have developed in this way for a very good reason. A tigress carrying young inside her will struggle to hunt. She becomes increasingly bulky, and her size and weight slow her down. She has no one to help her find food, and so, to help her survive, the pregnancy is as short as possible.

A HIDING PLACE

A tiger is a secretive animal at the best of times. When a tigress is about to give birth, she becomes even more secretive. She will find a safe place, with plenty of cover, so she can hide from meat-eating predators. In a mountainous area, she will find a gap between the rocks where she cannot be seen. The tigress is not only hiding from predators while she gives birth. She needs a place to hide her cubs when they are newborn.

The tiger and tigress will stay together for a few days, and then the tiger will be ready to move on.

The Family Life of Tigers

A tigress usually has two to four cubs, although some tigresses have been seen with as many as six cubs in their litters. The newborn cubs, which are about the size of fully grown pet cats, are completely helpless. At first, their eyes are not open. They are born blind and toothless, and, for the first few weeks, they will spend all their time drinking milk from their mother and sleeping.

EARLY DAYS

For the first couple of months, the small cubs are in great danger. At times, the mother must leave the cubs unprotected so that she can go hunting and get food.

While she is away hunting, other meat-eating hunters in the area, such as bears or packs of wild dogs, may attack the cubs. A mother tigress keeps her cubs safe by hiding them. She will have

The best way of keeping tiger cubs safe is to keep moving them from place to place.

The tigress changes from being a solitary animal to being a loving mother, playing with her cubs and teaching them all she knows.

a number of dens around her territory, and she will move the cubs at regular intervals. Usually, she picks up each cub with her mouth and carries it by the scruff, or loose skin, of its neck. Sometimes, she picks a cub up gently around its midsection. Either way, the tigress will pick up each cub in turn and carry it to a new, secret place.

When a tigress has cubs, she changes from being a solitary animal, which has only to look after itself, and becomes one of the most devoted mothers in the animal world. She looks after her cubs from the moment they are born until they are about fifteen months of age, when they are ready to look after themselves in the wild. In spite of all her care, usually only one cub in every litter will survive to become an adult.

The mother tigress **nurses** her cubs until they are about eight months old, although they will start to eat increasing amounts of meat from five months of age.

THE FATHER
People used to think male tigers did not play any part in raising their young. By studying tigers in the wild, scientists have found that a father tiger may defend a tigress and her cubs from other male tigers. He may also share a kill with a tigress and her cubs. A male may have a number of families in his territory, and he will spend a little time with each family unit.

25

The Tiger Cubs Grow Up

Tiger cubs are not born knowing how to hunt. A tigress must teach her cubs all the skills they will need to hunt and to survive in the wild.

LEARNING THROUGH PLAY

As the cubs grow older, they spend longer periods outside the den. They are very playful, creeping up on each other, pouncing, and having wild chases. The cubs are having fun, but they are also learning to use their bodies and to perfect the skills they will need when they start hunting.

When the cubs are three to four months old, the mother tigress will allow them to go with her on hunting expeditions. The cubs watch from a distance, learning from everything they see. When the cubs are about twelve months old, they must put their new-found

To begin with, the cubs are allowed only to watch their mother hunting.

Young tigers test their skills and build their strength by play-fighting.

hunting skills to the test. To begin with, the tigress provides the cubs with smaller animals to practice on. A tigress may wound a prey animal and then give it to the cubs to finish off. The cubs will then try stalking small animals. Many hunts end in failure in the early days, but, in time, the cubs become skilled hunters. At this point, they become less reliant on their mother for food.

GOING SOLO

When a tiger can hunt alone, it is time to move on. The young tigers will roam farther away from their mother, still keeping within her territory and staying in touch through scent messages and by roaring. Occasionally, they will return to share a kill with their mother, moving on again after a couple of days. When a group of tigers come together, they are known as a "streak" or an "ambush" of tigers.

A young tigress may find a territory close to her mother. A male has a far harder time. To begin with, he will spend his life on the move, wandering between territories and keeping out of the way of other male tigers. It is only when he has grown bigger and stronger that he will be ready to challenge another male and establish his own territory. Many males do not survive long enough to achieve this goal.

Tigers and People

The tiger is one of the most magnificent animals on Earth, but tiger numbers have fallen so much that they are under serious threat of extinction. Nine different types of tigers used to exist. Now, three types have died and will never be seen again. Of the six remaining types of tigers (the Bengal, the Indochinese, the South China, the Amur, the Malayan, and the Sumatran), the South China tiger is nearly extinct, with only twenty to thirty left in the wild.

FALLING NUMBERS

At the beginning of the twentieth century, there were 100,000 tigers in the wild. Now, there may be no more than 5,000. Why has the tiger, which has no natural enemies in the wild, suffered such a decline? The question can be answered in one word — people.

People have come into conflict with the tiger in many different ways. As people have developed land for homes, farming, roads, railroads, and mining, they have

At one time, people thought it was a great achievement to shoot a tiger living in the wild.

taken away the tiger's hunting grounds. The number of prey animals has also fallen, making it harder for tigers to survive. As tigers struggled to find food, they came closer to settlements and started killing cattle and other livestock. This made the tiger an enemy of the local people and so they were shot in large numbers.

The tiger also faced danger on another front. For many years, big-game hunting was a popular pastime, and shooting a tiger was seen as the greatest achievement of all. The tiger has also been hunted for its skin and for parts of its body, such as its bone and its whiskers, which are sometimes used in **Chinese medicine**.

MAN-EATERS
There have been many stories of man-eating tigers, which have spread fear and panic among people living in tiger country. In fact, a tiger will rarely attack without reason. It is only when a tiger is very old or is wounded and cannot hunt prey animals that it may be a threat to people.

The tiger needs wilderness areas where it can live undisturbed.

A BRIGHTER FUTURE?
We now understand the ways of the tiger, and laws now protect tigers in the wild. Unfortunately, there are very few wild areas left where tigers can live. Even though the tiger is in great danger of extinction, it is still hunted by **poachers**, who make big money by selling body parts for Chinese medicine. We have already lost three types of tigers. We must act now or it will be too late to save the last remaining tigers.

Glossary

ambush: a surprise attack by a predator that has been hiding

antiseptic: preventing infection

boundaries: the edges of a territory

camouflage: appearance colored and marked so that it blends in with the surroundings

canine teeth: teeth used for biting and killing

carcass: the body of an animal that has been killed

Chinese medicine: an ancient form of medicine that sometimes uses parts of an animal (such as the tiger's whiskers) to help cure patients

cover: trees, plants, and bushes where an animal can hide

evolved: changed form over generations

extinct: no longer alive

flehmen response: an action of the mouth that allows a tiger to pick up as much scent as possible

incisor teeth: teeth for cutting and tearing meat from bones

Jacobson's organ: a scent center in the roof of the tiger's mouth

mammals: warm-blooded animals that have hair and give birth to live young

molars: teeth for chewing meat

neutral territory: land that is not claimed by one individual or group

nurses: feeds a baby mammal with milk it sucks from its mother's body

poachers: people who illegally hunt animals

predators: hunters that kill other animals for food

pregnant: carrying an unborn baby inside until it is time to give birth

premolars: teeth for slicing and chewing meat

prey: the animal chosen by a predator to hunt and kill

rival males: two male animals competing with each other to mate with a female of their species

solitary: lives and hunts alone

species: animals that are classified as a single, related group

stalk: to creep up on a prey animal

territory: an area where an animal lives and hunts, which it will defend from other animals

tigress: a female tiger

victim: a chosen prey animal

More Books to Read

101 Facts About Tigers. 101 Facts about Predators (series). Julia Barnes (Gareth Stevens)

Tiger Rescue: Changing the Future for Endangered Wildlife. Firefly Animal Recue (series). Dan Bortolotti (Firefly Books Ltd)

Tigers. Big Cats (series). Victor Gentle & Janet Perry (Gareth Stevens)

Tigers. Our Wild World (series). Gwenyth Swain (Northwood Press)

Tigers: Striped Stallkers. Wild World of Animals (series). Adele Richardson (Bridgestone Books)

Web Sites

Bengal Tiger Pictures
www.bengaltigers.com/

Kids for Tigers
www.kidsfortigers.org/tigersden/allabttigers.php

National Geographic for Kids
www.nationalgeographic.com/kids/creature_feature/0012/tigers.html

Save the Tiger
www.savethetigerfund.org/Directory/kids.htm

Tiger Quiz
www.worldwildlife.org/fun/quizzes/tigers/

Publisher's note to educators and parents: Our editors have carefully reviewed these Web sites to ensure that they are suitable for children. Many Web sites change frequently, however, and we cannot guarantee that a site's future contents will continue to meet our high standards of quality and educational value. Be advised that children should be closely supervised whenever they access the Internet.

Index